A girl with a Fro

Black love and other poetic debauchery

Lyrical Paradigm

Table of Contents:

This book is dedicated to everyone who ever believed in me, given me a stage, a mic, or even just a chance.
I love you.
Thank you for loving me.

Girl with a Fro

Often times asked if my hair is real,
Because black girls don't really have hair.

I feel, like maybe there is some confusion.
Conclusions based on theory assumed right.

Let me, prove you wrong.

Black Girl Hair:

Nappy
Kinky
Curly
Long
Short
Wavy
Straight

All good hair.

Often times asked if my hair is real,
Because Black girls don't really have hair.

Yet, here I am,
Black!

Signed:
Girl With a fro

Droplet

We meet again, just you and I

we need to chat
I know there are some specific details you lack,
and perhaps, you will find them other places,
I just want to make sure you see the beauty in me that I see in
you
I won't judge for what you do
but pleasure is not real.

I watched you be exhumed from the other room
I followed you
slide down your spine for a birds eye view
ice cold your veins,
leaving traces of lipstick on the skin
and he, he doesn't even know us,

You and I
he doesn't know the pain hearts have been led through
how I appeared only when you needed me,
sank into your skin to remind you,

You wasted time
all you had to do was ask me to guide you
force me to pay attention to special mentions
he can't touch you like I do

yet you still allow his touching

you wasted me, let me drip past knees,
once I hit the ground I know that's the end of me
I hope you remember me before I leave.....

Black breastmilk

The first time you felt salvation,
The very first time you felt whole
Elaborated in a drunken stupor

Your white skin revived from this fountain of youth
Carried on backs
The same backs you pulled from seams
Whipped into submission
Suckled from queens

Did you see god when you saw her?
When you thought of her brown skin pressed against
fevered foreheads,
Did you ever wonder why after she gave you life you were
forced to hate her?
Did you ever even say thank you?

How does it feel?
Knowing that in her life she created her own demons
Molded them from clay
Breathed herself into them for protection
Whispers their prayers with her own
Watched them grow
Nurtured them
Taught them
Died by their hands

Did you ever try to save her?
Was she too far beneath you?

Tell me, how does it feel to hate yourself?

Why Love

I remember clearly when you laid yourself upon me,
ones never forget, love
I see the future you left right behind you
but you run way too fast for truth to find you.

Love, why you love so slow?

why you stall grown with lost hope
I hoped you would let me lead you,
we make love,
the same as I love you
I...love your particular brand of bullshit
you hold me down, so I don't forget to stand up,

Why love, do you want to break me?

Why do you tug heart strings loose,
un-mendable unmentionables
love you keep me talking
spilling my blood on sheets,
tell you our story to jog your memory

Love, why you love like that?

Bitter sweet kisses of wet yesterdays,
it rained monsoons when you left
How do you love free so tightly?
You leaving me wanting love
burning bridges to get to you,
Love don't run,
tip toe light on thin lines
border my nations
elixir to my shores
you make waters run cool against coasts
archenemy to horizons
I keep you close but you distance me love

Love, why do you affect me?

Confuse my senses
you fill my sight
linger in sunbeams
beauty tastes great on you
but why love,

Why you love confusing?

You labyrinth my todays
an I chase you into yesterday's
only now exists
you felicity butterfly wings,
We make love sick
tickle tingles with feathered tips of weakness, love
you strength me
love, I....heart you
symbolic, pure, unrequited
you require little upkeep
Yet you keep me up,

Why love do you wake me?

Fill my sleep with reality when I'm awake,
please leave me still
dancing in winds you blow on kisses
grooving back and forth in arms wrapped me

Why you move me, love?

make me giddy love
smiles of thick eyelashes
why you leave soon
go ready to quick return
joystick my emotions
master boards on stairways to heaven
captured Queens await arrivals
defeat the fight with fists of you
absolute my missions

Just to love me like this,
make me whole in parts
but why love?

Why you love like this...

Into Me....

He wants to be into me,
like stretch marked skin,
Deeply in, he wants to show me while he gets to know me.
His integrity to my voice he wants to introduce me,
induce me then speak deeper in to me
he wants to train my name to fight battles on the tip of his tongue
and when he's done,
the neighbors know my title, every single one.

I want to be the vinyl he lays his track on,
then sing in soprano while his bass bangs my back gone
he wants to drink of my soul the essence of my innocence
then fill me back up till I'm infinite,
Repeat every sin I ever committed
then repent to him
he wants to kiss the tips of my dignity
because he is digging me
he wants to know my intuition
so he submits to my vision
he wants to make me his mission
so he follows my tweets to see if my sheets become the topic of his
unfinished business
he wants me whole and complete.

He wants to be beyond deep
he wants to be pauper and slave, like the grave under the grave
he wants to see if in me he can be saved.
I can save him
he wants to be the rib from which I came from,
he wants his mental to meet my brain,
make him insane,
like 2 voices 1 at a time but they sound the same,
I'm in love with his idiosyncrasies

the perfect blend, he's awe and I some,
so he's always synced with me.

He wants the reason I live to him due
he wants to feel my heartbeat with the tip of his truce
his honesty dance to the beat of my tune
he wants to be moon
and I the sun he reflects
see when we connect
he wants to be more than best
he wants to be great
and make me the taste
his buds can't stand to waste.

He wants to be low down in my up hi
like gravity in an upside down sky
I told you he wanted to be deep, did you think it was a lie?
I just, want him to be my guide
lead me to a better life,
be the reason I don't need to search,
I want him to nurture me till I'm full, then release me like after birth
show him what his path is worth
make him rich like million dollar chips in a gamblers purse.

He, wants me to be the ending of every race he's beginning
then meet in the middle so be both cross the line at the right time
like a tie, so we both winning.
he wants my fears to meet his consciousness
while his hands rub me unconscious, yes
he wants to explore me more
fight pain with love making when me an him war
he gets me punch drunk, so I forget what we beef for,
colors my rainbows when the wind blows
then gives me peace after each storm,
and we haven't even tipped the scale with the pack that he stores.

His voice is mighty when he speaks, so I'm sure to listen
and my gratitude adds a kiss to his extension, not to mention
how he wants to supply my wisdom
so he gives me brain that sends chills thru my nervous system
increase my dopamine with his stroke,
I mean, his dope
he takes me higher than most, so I call him the most high
he wants to be into me like wings of angels, fly
flow within my groove
dig my move
royal like my blues,
he wants to be the absence of light in all my hues so I can see even his
black is beautiful too
This king has something to prove.

He wants to be the funk in my right leg, I guess he got a love jones
he wants to be so deep he will give up everything he owns
just to live a double life as the marrow of my bones
it almost makes you wonder how much deeper he can go
he wants to be the reason I still grow
so he teaches me lessons I need to know,
like how to take this love slow
he wants it to last forever and not just for show
no lights and a stage, just me, him and our home
maybe a kid or seven, who knows.

He wants to write my legacy in hieroglyphics on my throne
be a part of my ancestry, place my crown on this queens dome
so I give him the keys to my heart, show him what ecstasy looks like when
a kings home.
I never worry if he roams, behind him I leave bread crumbs of my skins
tone,
so he knows where to go when his dreams gone,
that's why he calls me free dome,

I release the inhibitions that make he strong

I guess that's why he wants to be into me......

Invincible

This love is invincible,
that means that nothing can kill it,

God willing

If you're willing,
I understand that you have baggage your lagging along this journey
but don't worry,
I knew what you packed before you packed it,
I knew you were a package,
but I decided I'll manage
because I think you worth it
your so far from perfect, that its perfect
you make me nervous
have you not noticed,
how the slight knee shake makes it hard to focus
but it's too subtle to be seen by the average being,
you know what I mean.
No really, I think it's just silly carrying on this way,
Like before our destiny was written it wasn't meant to be,
but you been meant for me since I was 15,
the first wet dream this love made me
and it might sound crazy,
This love is invincible,
that means nothing can kill it,

God willing

If you're willing,
to let go of all those ill feelings the love before me left building,
and piling up in your system.
You're the victim,
forced to live a life u didn't understand,
where I wasn't in the plan,
now you can see where the story went bad.

You were searching for the answer to questions never asked,
a love you never had,
but I been holding it down for you
waiting patiently for you to see where it's at
to see we better than that,
hell, we can make it through anything,
your my personal superman,
this love takes a ride down Lois Lane,
see its nothing like you had or will ever have again
I been planning to the end
because I know
This love is invincible
that means nothing can kill it

God willing

If you're willing,
to see from the beginning I needed you
I was breathing you before you knew what breathing do,
the mold was broke when god was kneading you
he knew I was needing you,
so he infused me with your spirit so deep in me I been bleeding you,
Since my dreams had color I been dreaming u
just hoping that one day u see in me what I see in you
how I be for you,
because this love is invincible
that means nothing can kill it

God willing

If you're willing
to see past my imperfection
past my collections of misdirection
but I'm right the right path now, so no stressing
see, I stopped going left and made a Right at Mr. street
you're the road to a new me
a new free,
so when I say you, you know I mean we.
Here is what I see,
a path of universal collisions, star written missions
body numbing loving and we only just kissing

I know this love is invincible
that means nothing can kill it..

God willing...

And if you are willing.....

Samson Song

This king of mine,
with sweet chocolate brown skin an small brown eyes,
I see into his future,
I see his kingdom come,
from him dreadlock tip,
like clasped grips around twisted perfections,
he's perfect for me,
I sit him on thrones so fly,
I change his name in my phone to kites,
so with every text I get high,
He is global warming an central cooling,
and the things that he's doing when perusing this blue moon
manifestation,
got it all mixed up in my head.
Seems this history we made already is still new.
I know years have passed since I met you,
and the universe is persistent too.

I know that past life was to test you,
but you have the power to allow me to resurrect you...

This king knows what happens once a good girls gone bad,
so he keeps me that way,
He understands that my throne is not around his waist,
he knows by his side is my rightful place.
He sees in me more than he sees in himself,
but I... see him as majestic,
perfectly imperfect,
I would have no home if he left it,
that's why when he gave me his heart,
I kept it.

I weep while he is sleeping,
because I can't read his mind.

This kind of mine with sweet chocolate skin an beautiful brown eyes,
I desire to taste the very nature of his disguise,
he tells me I'm beautiful at my worst,
I know he lies.
He teaches me lessons in delectable delights,
an pleasures my sights when he licks his lips left to right,
this King is tight,
Even with faults I love with no spite,
he's my Mr. wrong when doing wrong is so right,
I want to be his mission in life.

This King of mine with sweet chocolate brown skin a small brown eyes.....

Master

Master, who paints you?

Who creates brilliant hues of green and the blues?
Slight purple auras of you?
Does he see the masterpiece he creates?
Does he see broad spectrum?
Like a trifecta of green emotions,
envious of his own creation?
Is yours a jealous god?
Covetous of his beloved?
It seems every brush stroke is mahogany dipped,
cherry lips, eyes of fires freshly lit,
Master, it's a mystery how you even exist.
How love making made him fill to the brim in his bliss
then whispers of life air fills lungs and you stand tall with small of
back kiss,
and he with a steady hand, meticulously carved brown canvas into
this.
Then with arms stretched declared you into existence with melody
shaded tints,
His textured falsettos, horns blows in highs and lows
But Master, who writes your notes?
All tone altos bearing thrones in bellows of baritones?
Who builds crescendos of cheekbones,
4 heartbeats in tune to make you whole, d sharp to chest flat,
flaxen facial fashion, pitch pure in black,
the average man can't even imagine that, so who master?
Who created that?
Who picture perfect in his own image, but only one you?
Casting cast aside from broken molds,
from your eyes to your nose,
Master!

How did you become so royal with soiled skin tones?
Your creator had to be a genius, how else would he know?
How could he sketch deja vu in future you have yet to live,
then make me from your rib?
It's like he started with the darkness to begin,
Then added the light when I walked in,
And you looked at me with alpha bright eyes,
I'm like, Master, how twinkles like starlight make you fly?
Surely your god is a merciful one.
How else would he be able to give you to the world to behold?
Described imperial with miracles, then christen you with all known,
But my how you grow.
Put you on display because you had to be shown. You must be art.
The way your yellow foreground bares back,
Ground brown cellulose at perfect Celsius
as if each cell in us, was made to blend
again and again.
You puzzle other pieces of these masters who, filled you with the
spirit of ancestors,
rain dance in your shadows.
These valleys shallow, range peak past cloud,
you mountain top high, does he see you from the sky?
Observer of his creation, is your god all seeing?
Maybe rested in the breast of your being, breathing,
living, agreeing with every decision.
Was your mold made with provisions?
Back of leg mole part of the vision?
Your see through soul so all who knows you knows your mission,
but master, There is still an over standing that I am missing.
How a creation so grand could be made by one man?
Tribes, classes, and troupes had to make you working,
God's body couldn't possibly be earthly,
And your Gods crossed galaxies, just knowing you would be perfect
and deserving,
You're Promised Land that I am determined to be earning.
The pleasure more is mine to you serving,
because you.......are more than worth it to worship.

Amen

One Million Kisses

I don't want to die until we've kissed a million times
one by one,
every moment to come,
here is to lips and chin, fingers and thumbs,
hoping to get lost at 899 and starting back over at one,
there is no limit to my limits
no boundaries to have me bound
just lost and found
you losing yourself in me,
my kisses making you found,
lets count to ten and you go hide,
I'll find your eyes,
behind glasses and walls
you build them up tall,
for me to count every brick and kiss them all
lend me your heart and watch how we fall,
don't be eluded by delusions,
this 1025th kiss is for inclusion,
collar bones, shoulder blades, anything moving,
no words can express what my lips keep proving,
kissing on your soul is soothing,
healing me second hand,
just a second man, there is still 2945 kisses to plan
lend me your 3rd eye, watch how we grow,
place my 3000th kiss on the dip of your cupids bow,
your eyelids, eyebrows, the tip of your nose,
maybe even double back because there is still so far to go,
lay 5197 on your heart beat,
pattern the rest based on how you breath,

slowly and steady in a constant stream,
drag my lips across your skin and still count while you dream,
9999 on thighs
belly button, rib cage, the moles around your eyes,
ear lobes, cheek bones, all of your fears, at least I'll try,
I prayed for you, and you came so I just don't want to die,
until we have kissed at least a million times......

Work

This seems more like mental slavery,
We all know this is NOT the only way made for we,
Made to believe in make believe,
Fairy tales of magic beans,
Glass slippers that didn't fit
They were never made for me,
No prince charming ever came for me,
No savior or device
Just another trap to live a pretend life,
Don't know you can make it if you never try
My grammar stay broken
Physically fit in knowledge
My history doesn't lie
I know we were made to be more, young Moor
Don't let your black be drowned out by direct deposits bi-
weekly,
Don't allow your name to reflected weakly
These are Gods in your mirror image, seek he
Heed the truths they are seeping,
You are everything you ever wanted, it just takes more seeing
More doing, more being
Less whining about whitening the kings and queens you see on
TV
The revolution will be televised,
And Love and Hip Hop is not what I am meaning,
Keep reading,
Give your young Kings the wisdom they will be needing
The road less taken is the one you will be leading
So take it, claim it, and rename it in your power
Don't let fear hold you down,
Dance wildly in sun-showers,

Let rain wash you clean
Let that be the only work you truly devour,
Not chained to a desk being clocked by the hour......

Your Kisses

Your kisses are mysterious,
Even in your absence,
Dripping memories like newly born blessing resurrected,
You kiss like, morning rain washes away last night's sins,
Even your good mornings spoke in a tone meant only for hymns,
Praise to the most high,
Glory be the way your lips pressed against mine,
You're the reason urban legends exist,
Courageous conquests of damsels in distress,
Must be a myth, but I can attest,
First hand, over heart, in allegiance,
Your kisses change understanding,
Make me believe in the unbelievable,
Wonder where your origin originated and by whom,
Because you could not have been birthed, you had to be brewed,
Slow simmered in glistening you toned stew,
With subtle hints of kush and mirr and the blues,
I am forced to know it is true,
Your recipe is one of a kind,
Made to quench pains with ease,
I take tablespoons of you even if I feel the slightest sneeze,
Remedy to any illness there could be,
I think I feel an ache coming on and tender suckles of bottom lips is
what I might need,
A double dose please,
Make no haste, because every moment we waste my weak is
increased,
Waiting to be spilled all over counter tops,
Licked up, don't waste none,
Because this medicine is good for you,
I'm just trying to figure out how to get sicker and keep taking you
longer
So I can properly thank you,
The way thanks yous should be known to you,

In a million kisses owed to you,
The affects must be true,
Just this touch creates visuals on blank walls
No ceilings, no floors,
I am not sure, but your black magic had to be crafted by a voodoo
priestess,
Hard to build a resistance,
Your spell has me bound, tongue tied,
Slurred sound,
You cause a whirl wind affect with kisses simple, from neck
Shoulders next, then to chest, belly button, thighs,
I wonder when you will take a rest,
When dread locs body from right to left,
Tummy muscles marked and stretched, preparing for bearing your
seeds,
Gods in the form of human beings,
Funny how your cupids bows are always aiming for me
Poisoned by the tip of your arrows, Eros,
Punished by the hands of the perfect sin,
Then using this kiss to revive me like Psyche,
You have got to be a scholar in the Greek arts,
Like Athenian candles, the way we spark,
Odysseys down Achilles when Trojans begin to spar,
Spartan in your last life, you got warrior in your heart,
You can even help it
It's just the way you were made
Every new kiss like magic
I'm starting to think you might be magician by trade
The way you follow like road maps the tracks of my tears
Abracadabra, and a tap of your wand to make them disappear
Erase them from my memory banks like they were never even there
Replace them with replays of nude scenes
Shadow dances on moon beams
You affect how being in the mood seems
I swear, in your smile I can see how the universe was made
How foundations around crescent moons laid
Every time we touch I wonder if it's too soon to say
I fell in love with your bravery
And even though you got me wrapped up in this mental slavery

It's like I want to be needed there, am I crazy?
If I am really that's fine,
I can only hope to be punished for my crime and forced to roam land
mines of your mind to serve my time
Being blown up would be my pleasure, as long as i get to keep you
here as mine
And as long as I get to kiss you one last time.....

The Truth about a Man

His silhouette is engraved deeply thru traces of tears we shed
together
His reflection mirrored images created in past tense
My earliest writings hieroglyphs etched into memories of long
nights and heroic conquests
He shining (k)nights definition
I only hope to be dipped in his glory
Draped on his most dynamic imagination
Drunk on his history
He pure intention
Masterfully carved, curb lined with guided direction
Earth tones stretched to skylines,
He dances moon energy and oxygen,
Maker of afternoon sun shine,
He fatherhood
First hand
Teacher of revolutions,
5 past 360,
Evolutions of brightest star,
Shimmering power
I always find myself staring,
Hoping to sink into his skin through tunnel vision
He what drowning feels like
Loss of breath
Unable to take in nothing other than he
I dream to be pleasured by his reaping
Sowed and saturated
Filled to brims
He divine revelations, 1:16
Completion
Invincible like immortality

He in my blood
He speak God fluently
Wisdom be his language
He easy learning
I revel in being taught
Ever willing pupil
Dilated minds
Blinding, like even in my absence I still see all of he
Imprinted on prayers
Blessed in the name of our sons,
Stamped first class ashe, as he.
His ascension gargantuan like baby steps.
Deliberate
He messy like jumping on beds and pillow fights
Trippy and colorful
He still only brown
Painted in beauty
I wonder what line he stood in to dipped,
Where the remains of his perfect mold are spread,
What other earthly parts are replicas of his creation
He genuine like glistening on oceans
Sun beams
Radiation
Affects my biology
He constant change,
We shapeshift,
Like clouds or fairy tales
He is happy endings after escape
Saved from the parents after working on railroads
All the livelong day
He written in hymn,
His songs don't rhythm
He Limerick.

Dear Future Husband #1

I know sometimes it's hard to find the words to what you want to tell
me.
Truthfully, I too am not that great at telling.
Even with all the nouns I know by heart, where to start becomes just a
little too far.
So I won't write you poetry
I won't recite lyrics that you already know from me
No metaphors,
No similes,
No didacting,
Instead I rather just tell you in actions without all the acting
Show you in fractions, because every little bit counts, down to the
smallest ounce of intention
I won't rely silly phonetics to display what I say, besides, who listens to
hearing anyway
My mama always said that seeing is believing, and believing is what
my hoping,
Hopping greedily in to knowing,
I know there is wisdom in having survived the test of time
There is loving in having tested minds, besides, who wants to be stuck
behind a disguise.
I only want you to see the real thing.
Get a clear vision of what real means and be willing to jump head first
without fearing,
There really is nothing to be afraid of.
There's a different kind of beauty in the roughness of the ways we
make love,
Even coal had to take a little pressure to become what diamonds are
made of
There are not enough words to describe our measures
no equation to divide our blended textures,
it won't be hard to add up what we subtracted to distract us, but don't
look back love,

We'll be seasoned with more than just salt pillars
we'll be perfected to taste, no preservative, and no fillers.
We'll share this classically organic dynamic, all that shit behind us, let
the past have it.
Let it be another man's treasure to find,
Consume their time,
While only we consume mine, because I can see past the walls you
build to hide.
I'll be patient working on it, one brick at a time, and I won't give up
when it gets hard either,
I got the tenacity of ten men in just one little finger
Just wait you will see
Please, when you tell me your dreams, don't forget to tell me the
things that hurt you,
The little ticks that irks you, these are the things I want to help you
work through.
There is nothing we can't solve together
I really mean anything and whatever
If it can get bad, please believe it can always get better.

For you, I promise never to give you a reason to question my loyalty.
Don't ever wonder if I appreciate you.
For me it's real easy to give you kingdoms to bow down to your royalty
You will never have to assume your purpose, see I met God when I
met you with certainty.
So don't become stressed with worrying.
I have you covered
You can find safety in the lines of my sheets for comfort
Read between them
Understand their meaning
Give them power in aloud reading, because they can only manifest in
your speaking.
I will always have a prayer with your name on it
Fill it with myself when I say it
Seal it with a kiss for protection from Heru, from the (a)mun in me to
the (a)she in you, and no,
I won't write you any fairy tales.
Instead tell tales of your totem
The way you were molded

The strength of your shoulders, the beauty from the eye of this
beholder.
You will have no choice but to live forever
There will be no punch lines nothing overly clever.

I can only show you what I know.
Reflect the god in you in my growth.
Constantly pledge you in oaths.
Just one heart and one soul.
One mind and one breath,
Whatever comes next, comes next,
I don't plan on regrets.
Only plans of falling asleep on chest and being right by your side if and
when things start to go left,
I am more than prepared to take it
Willing to fight with and for you until we make it, and we'll make it.
This is something I know,
I just have the hardest time finding the right words, so....
I promise,
I won't write you poetry,

Signed,
Imperfection

After being called a nigger by a white man...

I asked my white mom, why did you make me black?
She told me because, she was God.
Said she loved a black man named nigger, and became the target of
some hazing and shaming.
I asked her to explain it to me

She said, long before you knew me,
I knew black. I knew real black.
Black with arms that holds in every ray of light.

She said he was a sight to behold,
He glistened like gold,
Land mines of minds he seemed to know,
She said he once crossed shores of past lifetimes,
Shape shifted into her dreams one day before creation.

She told me,
She warned me of the day when because of them, my black would be
too much,
My power would be misunderstood.
She said she often calls me by name, but I could not hear it.
I had become deaf, white noise had drowned out my hearing.

She told me, but Black aint never been color blind,
aint never been so absorbed in its own light that it forgot to see
change coming.
She called me by name, Ashe.
Told me to say it before bed each night,
To wish upon stars for anything my heart desired,
She told me not to forget my black.
To let each time of day be the right time for dream chasing

She chased out any inconsistency.
Reminded me of wisdom and warm hugs,
More than to herself, she was the master of none

I asked her how she knew she was God?
How she rose up from concrete jungles, and sprouted wings?
She told me it was simple.
She woke up.
She said don't trust they stories, to many times they had been
rewritten,
She said, stop blocking the sun and stand in it
Read more, or better yet read less,
You been trained to read the wrong text,
Words are supposed to go from right to left,
There's only faces in your books,
Less plot twist, too much sex,
More hearts on sleeves than bare naked chests.
Where was the last place you looked for god?
Did you find me?
Was I wasting time looking for an answer no one ever questioned,
Every time you called my name did I pay attention?
Or was I consoling black grandmothers who black grand babies went
missing.
She asked me with such conviction,
Made me question my entire motive and mission.

She asked me, you wonder why they freed the slaves in June?
So they would never have to celebrate you in schools,
But Look what I taught you.
Let me show you a fool,
A man who claims wisdom but speaks the language of a slave tool,
Dig deeper, fine something closer to your roots,
Let me show you black.

I asked her, where she was when my black needed saving?
She looked me square in the eye,
With a heart beat in a rhythm just like mine,
She said, all over,
Those questions you have, I gave you the notions.
Those lessons you learned I wrote them
Those voices in the back of your mind I spoke them,
Before labia made you lady, I made you brown,
From dirt and sound.
She said, I'm the very reason you standing and living,
Just look at where you were and where I now have you positioned,
I knew, she was right, and later that night before I went to bed,
I saw god again,
I saw a different kind of beauty in all her melenated skin,
I kissed her hands, she kissed my forehead,
She told me, melanin gave me super powers.

So yeah, I know god, just well as I know black, and I am proud to be both.

Don't Fall For Me

I never asked you to fall
Mainly because I am no pit
More like a long haul,
Strap me to your carriage and carry me.
But only when I can't walk on my own.
Let it be known that all the metaphors for for-ever an for now's are
only for emphasis,
Four letters, in every four sentences.
Don't fall for me.
You should never fear landing.
I don't want to break you,
An right now my arms are not strong enough to catch fast pitches,
Stand up understand me.
Grow me
For that you will need plenty of light an space,
Feed me with small bits of your soul
A sprinkle of gold,
A pinch of intention
Watch how I get you lifted,
I'm opposite of dissention, so don't fall for me.
Save your bended knees,
Or be wounded warrior,
I need you linear, even if seated,
Move mountains Anu,
For these Naki come stomping.
We could never be so low that our screams become whispers
Heat always rises,
Teach me how to echo, I will yell it into the deepest seas,
Don't, be so lost in falling that you forget to climb the trees
There is forest behind those walls,
But if you cannot see it you will get lost
Abate, imbalanced, topple over
Never in my vain,
My name only reminded of heavens and stars
Galaxies out somewhere far,
Distant from extinction,

Don't be defeated, this is not a war.
I am no fighter,
Protector
Guardian, you can call me that instead
Don't expect to be deep
Unless you mean like light years
Past any prime, only Optimus
Trust me Jack, you will never fall down,
You crown will always be carried
Sway in the colors,
Flourish in the light
Remember your perfect spectrum is at eye level
Let's be even,
Parallel like train tracks,
When was the last time falling bridged a gap
Instead of that, let's be space less,
Defy gravity
Just whatever you do
Don't fall for me....

Maids Made Men

There once was a woman,
With her eyes she took the souls of men,
ripped them apart to repair them,
She was a healer,
Stripped them of all assumed past damages,
She was magic in the art of savages,
Drizzled with misconception,
She knew her superpower well,
She bathed in thoughts of conquer,
Although she was most drenched in divide,
One glance,
One slight of eye,
She had it,
But when she broke,
No one fixed her,
How selfish of her for being fragile,
Lucky for her she had dust busters under her
bustle,
She was also the cleanup woman......

What Growing Feels Like

She awakes
Broken from the mold of yesterday
Stretches to release from undergrown skin
She smiles
Expectant of great today's
Less worried about uncontrollable yesterdays
Tomorrow never seemed to bright
After noon,
She wonders what wonders will be wondered today
Passing time imagining a stronger imagination
She is breathing easy of no regrets,
She pats her face dry of last night's tears,
No more thoughts of what didn't go right and what she
wished would go wrong,
She breathes
One slow breathe in
She remembers living
She sees sunshine like path light
She leads a new today
She pushes covers exposing appendages intertwined
Loosen tight,
She stands,
Smiles again,
She still remembers loving,
Stretches again to shed the remainder of past,
She smiles.......

Dear Future Husband #2

Come take a walk with me.
Through secrets gardens of peace and knowing,
the ones where no flowers grow, but growth is always occurring
look me in my face.

Find comfort there.
Find strength in locs of curls of hair
I put them there for you to discover.

Leave behind your wonder.

Just breathe
Now before you let go, say to yourself real slow,
I Am God.
Watch how that smile spreads across,
Rest your cape on the chair.
Dip your feet into shallow pools of joy and step.
Fall asleep in the trees every night.
Bend down when you listen to the grass grow.

Exhale
In this garden, there is no worry, because I have weeded it out,
Planted new seeds and sowed them in your honor,
rest upon them my sweet.
Let dreams make you find what you thought you lost but never did,
it's always been here.
I always can see it.
I have no problem showing it to you,
recite and chant, weed out, replant.

Rest

Find no wonders into tomorrow.
Find no wonders into what will.
Now, there only is.

Rest upon my cape for a change,
I just had it dry cleaned.

Becoming a Butterfly

She emerges from darkness dragging yesterday's
trash behind her.
Hoping the secrets leaking from her hefty bag can
be left not to find her,
She opens the gate to her present to find her
garbage can,
Pauses to rethink her plan,
Only to go back to her first mind,
She finds, her story not ending, and with lower
back pains beginning,
She lifts from weak knees,
Opens the lid of past life, an drops in her burdens
low beneath the surface,
Even stops to notice the dry face that tears don't
penetrate,
She demonstrates composure,
Exposure to the elements have left her with a
solemn choice, to let go, or fall over,
So she lifts
Conquers, delivers an she threw
She lowers the lid
Wipes her hands of residue
She smiles...

She is now free....

Mount Olympus Chronicles: The death of Zeus

He was my everything.

Everything he wasn't I tried to make him.
I would take him to heights higher than any God could ever create him
and when those other whores tried to break him,
he held my hand tighter by his side.
He knew he had a queen who in just one move replaced an erased them.
We made good music.
We made slow jams like old school dusties.
He loved me just like Aretha said he would, and Franklins didn't matter to Mr. Feelgood.
He cured my ailments with the first kiss.
I first wished, he would impregnate me with perfection just so I could rebirth his.
Show him what his worth is.
We were good together,
He was my down dude, so when I was feeling cocky and rude, he just sat and watched me
then climbed up on top of me and just....watched me.

We were cataclysmic
Determined and rhythmic, when he spoke I couldn't help but to listen in digits.
Counting how the ways he said he loved me in his sentence
I couldn't stand to be without him for even minutes
This man was poetry, masterfully carved like his bars, but I built him a prison.
I left him written in stars in a universe where he wasn't a part.
We rushed in to soon, ended before we could really start.

I never gave him a chance when he gave me his heart.
I loved him whole, but not fully.
Completely, but not enough to love him more.
Sometimes nights I spent wishing for the same feelings we had before,
but I was too slow being his friend and too quick closing the door.

Now looking back I can see what his pieces were for...

79th and Cottage Grove, A Love letter

Dear 79th,

Every day I get lifted in my sky high view and I watch you,
An although your skies blue,
I swear you make red boil down,
I wonder what could have happened to turn u around.
I can tell by your structure
You were loved by another
Maybe father and mother,
But somewhere between birth an becoming colored, you lost it,
You became lame in the name of Taylor an Leakes,
Home for the children of the weak
How many feet did it take to walk over you?
How many dreams died in the fire that smoldered you?
Made you wasted in white daggers, Glass blown diaries,
Syphoned dissatisfaction, When did it not matter?

Every single day,
I sit in my cloud an watch you fade
Sirens get lower, voices pitched for its replace,
With each blurred face, I wonder,
when sagging pants and nail shops full of babies became your
favorite past time.
I remember last time, the last night we spent before in a past life.
I can't recognize for blue and white lights,
Late nights aren't like they used to,
Abused abusers abused you
Corruption misused you
Scapegoated your presence just to lose you,
I hope you become saved,
An your children raised,
An your shine becomes what your worth,
Regular people would be amazed.

Auf Wiedersehen.........

Untainted Love

The broken hearts on your shadows warned me about you before I

ever knew your name, love,

I could tell by the crooked smiles one too many strokes has bogged

you down.

Your walk is what really gave it away.

Limp like your Rose had broken one to many thorns.

I saw you try to smile when my warmth greeted you.

I could tell you were not used to my kind.

Had never encountered such an extra-terrestrial,

Unknown was what you were good at.

My Black Mom vs My White Mom

My Black Mom / My White Mom

Get yo damn hands off that! / No no, don't touch that!

Set yo black ass down! / Please sit down.

Negro Please! / No sir/ma'am.

Don't make me slap the hell out of you! / No, please stop!

Do your chores! / Go outside so I can clean up!

Don't let anyone put their hands on you! /Don't fight.

Just rinse it off! / Don't eat off the floor.

Don't waste food.   / If you don't like it, throw it away.

Read every book. / Read the bible.

Question everything. / Don't ask so many questions.

Live how I tell you. / Live how you want.

Come home. / Come home safe.

I love you. / I love you.

Haiku Taboo

Walking through the Grass,
Almost stepped in shit two times,
Would you look at god!

      I go pee freely,
    It cost too much to be free
      I pay for water

          He said, I love you
        He couldn't have meant it
         Don't believe the hype

He be giant step
I be pretty dirty dress
And he still chose me

     Four Letters broke me
    Two letters brought me right back
      All I got is me

Be Open with her
Don't just disappear into air
She will not forget

James Circus

It's 12am,

Step right up to see the greatest show on North Ave,

because earth is small from this side of town at night,

yellow houses house yellow babies.

To your left, the first landmark ancient Kings would search for

queens,

white diamond filled nostrils, burn bridges of vodka and tonic,

it was always a blue light,

they say you can still hear the whispers when lions sleep.

To your right, rainbow dreams of rainbow children,

pots melting of lethal injections,

be sure to mind the signs,

Don't feed the animals, they will attack,

and it's not always wise to attack back,

but look at the smiles on the beasts,

joy on their backs,

they love like love is familiar in concentration camps,

they try to concentrate on having each other,

a little sister, 3 big brothers,

part time mother,

they want to be just like her,

so they pretend to tend bar,

just listen to the sounds of the happy singing,

Who's bad?

Next stop on this moon walk is simply thrilling,

its 2:45,

this is typically where REM sets in,

pay attention to purple stars,

there will be a pop quiz at the tours end,

hold your breath,

as not to breathe in the stench of fresh pipes,

lies, icy blue eyes,

kisses, tears,

look out overhead for falling fears,

if you are hit, side effects may vary,

here you'll enjoy the best cakes and pies,

the biggest smiles one can conquer,

straight ahead you will notice the light getting brighter,

like suns growing wiser,

moving faster,

each blink a minor disaster,

amazing the tenacity of a bastard,

hold on to your seats for this next fast forward of the ride,

you can even close your eyes,

some things don't require to be spied,

but in just a short time, rise and shine,

blue waters cover golden shores,

dances of tribes,

rain songs and more

but let's stop for a moment to let others on,

step right up to see the greatest show on these streets

watch your step as not to step on the pride of immortal

please take your seats..

Love of Hemlock

Him kiss morning dew from cheeks bones before he goes to earn

his bread,

Him sweat back, break spine an mind to keep his seeds fed,

He's a gardener, a carpenter, a leader an a friend,

Moses, Samuel, Samson, an Jesus could learn a thing or two from

him,

He softens blows with blows of wind,

Covering fears,

Him fears nothing,

him wisdom eyes and ears,

He see future in past tense, he was born in lightyears,

Him love galaxies too, deep be black holes,

Yet somehow he knows when to give gravity control,

Him so down to earth, clouds and rain envy he,

They, slow descent an get lost in trees, but the forest him still see,

Him masterpiece graphite, led by him speech,

Him drop jewels college ruled when him teach,

Stroke notes on throats, across covers an sheets,

Stand up, stretch out, repeat,

Him shimmy shake love jones, tip of head, middle, feet

Front face back, seams where him black meet,

Him work of art artwork, sculpted from molds broken,

Him word spoken from gods, life speak, against odds,

him road less taken, so him more scars,

Him sights worth seeing, him worth stars,

To him life worth giving, mine if he asks,

Anything for he, him ford tough, built to last,

Him the alpha an last,

beginning of the greatest end.........

Dear Mommy,

Its only befitting in your touch I found knowing. Traced cracked crevices of your hand print, stained glass windows of the road ahead, I found imagination in our rebellious art. I wondered sometimes how your veins bleed so cold on warm nights, kissed foreheads, I knew you would be a star someday. I knew your afterthoughts would always resonate in my brain, I knew you would always be watching. I found, curiosity in your eyes, icy blue, blurred edges, I imagined they would play your thoughts out for me to see, and I watched them like old movies on projector screens, they always came out in color. I wondered how many times your slightly tanned porcelain hand faded in winters palm Persephone, you would often say leaving home most nights was hell. I wondered how many seeds had you swallowed, what was your penance. To me it seemed like each spring you would bring another garden to carry, I sometimes wondered if your arms got tired and why the monkey on your back never grabbed a load. You used to tell me you were always leaving because you worked hard to feed me, I wondered while you were away if you ever snuck in to see me, whisper dreams in my ear while I was sleeping, but the dreams I was dreaming taught something darker, an alternate meaning, a starker contrast to the image you painted, thick eye brows furrowed explaining, there will always be things dreams never teach you...love.

In your existence I found understanding. Finding life lines thru pipe lines, I know now, you cried when you were alone. Your written history told me so, an even in the things you never wrote, but I read brands. Written by your past, on arms that screamed to be free, you were me. Impressions you made to leave, you taught me which path I was meant to lead, Now, I know what happens to a dream deferred. I now know what happens to blonde haired little girls, too beautiful to love properly, probably never learning what it means. I saw her in every photo I kept in my memory banks, there are only 3. I am now very familiar with the tune the caged bird sings, we harmonize in unity for your release.

I guess I should also tell you, in your arms I found self. I could hear you sometimes whisper under your breath that I was the greatest thing that ever happened to you. But I still wondered, what happened to you? What curse by day caused your demise, what silly little love song did you sing when you walked the streets at night? I bet it was a slow jam. You taught me my skin was mine to claim, darker than yours, but still same. You would often tell me of the origin of my name, how you gave it to me because it was your favorite word to say, Mums is what you called me. And I made sure to call you before bed every evening. Stories over the phone, with a background hint of lighter flicks, Newport burns and deep breathing, you would tell me tall tales on short nights. Long stories of your short lived life, I know that your presence was never in vain. Even on days I thought I would never see you again, when I least expected it is when you came.

In your presence I came to know life. Watching you dress for work, I realized no high heels, but yours seemed to be the remedy, the cure for the pain life caused you, hate life taught you, but in us you found a new reason to keep going, to keep moving even if your pace was slower than the rest, and because of that, I cannot give up. You taught me strength in your failures, wisdom in your mistakes, and peace in your chaos. I found solace in your hugs and wonder in your smile. In your life, I came to know truth.

In your sickness, I found resurrection. Filled from lungs to heart to brain, it was as if the cancer traced the path for me to follow. And I did, religiously. Re-birthed by your absence, I know now, you will always be present. As long as you consume thoughts, and speak life into nightmares, I know you are always with me. I wish upon you each night, star. Your twinkle is brighter now than ever before, and I, love to bask in your suns reflection.

Looking back Sally Ann, I must say, you and I came a long way, and I wouldn't change it for the world. I miss you every day old lady!

Your favorite girl,

Mums

Made in the USA
Lexington, KY
09 August 2017